From Within a Broken Heart

By Emily Schaubeck

To all sick minds struggling in a world not
meant for us

Trigger Warning

The contents of this book include poems and prose, as well as other writing excerpts, by Emily Schaubeck during a time of great distress and emotional turmoil.
(aka High School)

Suffering with severe longterm clinical depression, as well as other diagnoses, Schaubeck writes about the deeper issues and conflicts of the human condition.
The contents of this book can be described as…

Hopeless
Sad/Depressed
Suicidal Ideation
Loss/Grief
Death
Loneliness
Etc.

Emily Schaubeck

ALL THAT YOU DON'T SEE

Deep inside there is someone
who can't really find themself
…
Because deep inside there is someone
who wants to be someone else
…
Deep inside there is someone
who is always angry and sad
…
Because deep inside there is someone
who thinks they might be mad
…
Deep inside there is someone
who dreams like there is no tomorrow
…
Because deep inside there is someone
who is always filled with sorrow

Emily Schaubeck

You may say that I am King
and one might think
I know everything

…

You may say I make no mistake
and I will have you know
that theory is fake

…

You may say I am a petty man
with no care in the world but my own

…

And you may believe I am a selfish man
with a carriage of silver and gold

…

But what you don't know
is what really matters
that I do all in my power
to keep my kingdom un-shattered

…

I sacrifice my blood
and I would give my life

…

I will lead you into battle
with my hand on the knife

Emily Schaubeck

In the clouds is where I am
During most of my time
…
Where there is grass
And trees and hills
A place where the wind chimes chime
…
Far away is where I am
Where no one will ever know
…
With birds and bees
And all the beasts
A place where the river flows
…
And although my body is here
One soul among the crowds
…
And although you may not think much of me
My mind is up in the clouds

Emily Schaubeck

CONNECTIONS

From the light there is shadow
From the shadow there is darkness
From the darkness there is the moon
From the moon there are tides

. . .

From the tides there are waves
From the waves there are fish
From the fish there is food
From food there is life

. . .

From life there is death
From death there is night
From night there is day
So from darkness there is light

Emily Schaubeck

SEE YOU IN HEAVEN

Soft Grass
Blue Sky
Puffy White Clouds
…
By a Lake
Under a Tree
With a Little Sigh
…
Gentle Music on a Hill
This is Where You Will Be
…
A Place of Peace
Up in the Sky
A Place Right Next to Me

Emily Schaubeck

One lonely soul among all the rest
One always a failure when it comes to the test
One dying flower among a bouquet
One that is wilted and close to decay

…

One lonely fish among a school in the sea
One always sad, while others play happily
One dying ember among logs aflame
One that is weak, Oh what a shame

…

One lonely rock among grains of sand
One always too dull and never too grand
One dying wolf among his own pack
A love for him, was what they all lacked

Emily Schaubeck

There was a boy I used to know
his name was Michael Brown
we used to laugh and play together
for he was such a clown

…

We went so many places
and oh I loved him so
but now he is just a memory
someone I used to know

…

Now many years have flown by
his image lost inside my head
and when I look back to that little boy
I see that Michael Brown is dead

Emily Schaubeck

I had to grow up before my time
Something most will not understand
I had to adjust to what you learn later on
a pebble surrounded by sand

...

I had to learn the way of the world
at such an early age
and I had to learn to take care of myself
yet trapped within this cage

...

I had to learn to see the world
through many different eyes
I also had to fight my fights
despite my own small size

...

And nothing that I do or say
can fix what they have done
so I must quietly sit here
and wait for the rising sun

Emily Schaubeck

SHATTERED WINDOWS

Shattered windows, Broken Doors
how many walked these creaky floors
a leaky roof that lets the rain in
three fourths dry until it pours

…

Tattered drapes
a blood stained wall
I would hate to see you fall
sole purpose it has and always will
the only reason they still stand tall

…

Used up furniture
and old photographs
holding onto memories that would
make you laugh

…

But those times have passed
dark shadows come
the house wants to crumble
before it is done

…

But no matter the struggle
no matter the pain, the house will still be there
although his heart has been slain

Emily Schaubeck

Although you may think you know
much about me
I can say that you are wrong
because I am not like the others out there
for I can hear your song

...

The eyes are walls of glass
the mind is an open book
you cannot hide your soul from me
all I have to do is look

...

So when you are caught in a hollow gaze
here is what I see
a child lost within a maze
so come and follow me

...

Come and follow me
reach out and take my hand
for I will love you
and I will lead you
from this dead an shadowed land

...

—>

It is all going to be okay in the end
until then we must endure
come and I will show you the way
I will show you what I fight for

...

So when I see you staring out
I know and understand
all that you are going through
so come and take my hand

Emily Schaubeck

Courage is Crystal
Bravery is Gold
The heart in them
Must all be bold
…
Anger is Red
Orange is Joy
With their spirit
You cannot toy
…
Yellow is Strength
Beauty is Green
So many things
Their eyes have seen
…
Peace is Blue
Purple is War
We keep taking
More and more
…
Silver is Purity
Grace is Bronze
Struggling now
To break their bonds
…
White is Death
Human is Black
Respect for them, is what we lack

Emily Schaubeck

THE MASK

Behind this face, you may see a man
strong and lean, and sort of tan
with short dark hair, and teeth that gleam
full of pride for he had a dream

…

At ten he watched a lot of cartoons
they opened his mind, with their silly tunes
fifteen brought the boy, sport and school
they taught him not, to break any rules

…

Some time passed, and twenty five came
upon being a soldier, he was never the same
from then until thirty, the best years of his life
because he had met, his darling wife

…

A son and two daughters, brought joy to his heart
although during their time, his dear wife
had to part

…

And then came the day, that marked sixty years
he didn't waste time to shed any tears
his eyes now are fading
and his children are grown, they continue the
dream with young of their own

—>

Now covered in wrinkles, and hair stained white
soon will be my turn, to go towards the light
but for now I must sit here, sit all alone
sit and endure, Your uppity tone

…
I've watched many live
I've watched many die
I simply watch as life passes by

…
But behind this face
you may see a man
forever young
He is, who I am

Emily Schaubeck

THE THINGS I WONDER

What if the ocean was neon pink?
What if ships were supposed to sink?
…
Why is the earth shaped like a sphere?
What is wrong with a square?
Why can't a moose look like a turtle?
…
I don't really think that's fair

Emily Schaubeck

THE TRUE ENEMY

There is so much that you don't know
about the world that has come and go
…
So much you did not see or hear
So much death, sorrow, and fear
…
So much pain, and so much war
why can't things be like before?
…
When life was simple, pure and new
the world was a better place
until they fell to hunger and greed
it is but an endless chase
…
Turning upon one another killing as they go
facing sister against brother
killing all the wrong foe
…
And then I stop and think to myself
what will become of us?
Because what all people fail to see
will be our own worst enemy

Emily Schaubeck

Today I am Happy
and I do not know why
at may even seem
as if I can fly

…

No insults
No bee stings
No mean crocodile
could ever demolish
my big toothy smile

…

What typically irks me
today, has no effect
all dark heavy rainclouds
bowed down in respect

…

No cuts
No breaks
come bring on the pain
my cheerful spirit
will never be slain

…

For today I am happy
took a push and a shove
then I realized my dear
I have fallen in love

Emily Schaubeck

VOICES

Below and Above, there are voices
the ones you cannot see
Below and Above, there are sorrows
the ones that appear to me

...

Through the rocks
Through the trees
Through the winds they fly
Through tearful waters
Through empty fields
Through the Northern Sky

...

Below and Above, there are whispers
the ones you cannot hear
Below and Above, there are secrets
the ones that we may fear

...

Through the eyes
Through the soul
Through the winds they creep
Through every mind
Through every heart
Through nights they do not sleep
—>

Below and Above, there are cries
the ones you cannot feel
Below and Above, there are screams
of the ones that are not real

...

Through the shadows
Through the dark
Through the winds they go
Through here and there
Through everywhere
It is this, you do not know

Emily Schaubeck

People think that I am stupid
They think that I don't try
They all assume that I don't care
When inside I want to die
…
People think that I am tough
And that I am worry free
They all think that I am strange
And nothing bothers me
…
People think it all comes easy
They think that I am mad
But what they cannot really see
Is that I am just really sad
…
Everywhere I go
No matter what I do
People turn and look at me
I bet even you

About the Author:

    Emily Schaubeck is a Chinese American Adoptee from New York, USA and this collection of works is a depiction of Schaubeck's life during her four dreadful years of high school. Suffering from longterm clinical depression, as well as other diagnoses, Emily has made it her point to share her story and words from the heart in order to help break the stigma of mental illness; as well as help others feel less alone in this world.